TO THE RESCUE!

Res Sea

Ar ld

WITHDRAWN

Raintree is an imprint of Capstone Global Library Limited, a company incorporated in England and Wales having its registered office at 264 Banbury Road, Oxford OX2 7DY – Registered company number: 6695582

www.raintree.co.uk
myorders@raintree.co.uk

Edited by Linda Staniford
Designed by Steve Mead
Picture research by Eric Gohl
Production by Victoria Fitzgerald
Originated by Capstone Global Library Ltd
Printed and bound in China

ISBN 978 1 474 71525 6 (hardback)
19 18 17 16 15
10 9 8 7 6 5 4 3 2 1

ISBN 978 1 474 71534 8 (paperback)
20 19 18 17 16
10 9 8 7 6 5 4 3 2 1

British Library Cataloguing in Publication Data
A full catalogue record for this book is available from the British Library.

Acknowledgements
We would like to thank the following for permission to reproduce photographs:
Alamy: Alan Dawson Photography, 9, David Wingate, 13, Jinny Goodman, 10, Ladi Kirn, 12, 22 (top), Tim Jones, 20, US Marines Photo, 17; DVIC: U.S. Coast Guard/Cutter Healy, back cover (right), 19, 22 (bottom), U.S. Coast Guard/Larry Kellis, 15, U.S. Coast Guard/PO2 Barry Bena, 5, U.S. Coast Guard/PO3 Ross Ruddell, 18; Getty Images: LightRocket/Pacific Press/Ibrahim Khatib, 21; Newscom: Image Broker/Jochen Tack, 6, Photoshot, 11, Photoshot/Angel Manzano, back cover (left), 7, 22 (middle), Photoshot/NHPA/Guy Edwardes, 4, REX/Kazam Media, 14, Stock Connection USA/Craig Lovell, 16, VWPics/Mike Greenslade, 8; U.S. Navy: Air Crewman 2nd Class Darien Durr, cover

Design Elements: Shutterstock

Every effort has been made to contact copyright holders of material reproduced in this book. Any omissions will be rectified in subsequent printings if notice is given to the publisher.

All the internet addresses (URLs) given in this book were valid at the time of going to press. However, due to the dynamic nature of the internet, some addresses may have changed, or sites may have changed or ceased to exist since publication. While the author and publisher regret any inconvenience this may cause readers, no responsibility for any such changes can be accepted by either the author or the publisher.

Contents

Rescue at sea 4

Rescue at the beach..6

What do lifeguards do?....................................8

What transport do lifeguards use? 10

What happens when there is an
emergency out at sea?....................................12

How are people rescued out at sea? 14

How do aircraft help rescue people at sea? ...16

What if lifeboats and planes can't
get there?..18

Making the world a safer place! 20

Quiz 22

Glossary 23

Find out more...24

Index 24

Some words are shown in bold, **like this**.
You can find out what they mean by looking
in the glossary.

Rescue at sea

The sea can be very **dangerous**. When the wind is blowing hard and the waves are very high, people can quickly get into difficulty at sea.

A boat's engine can break down, or a member of the crew may need **medical** help. There are different kinds of **emergency** services around the world that can help people who need to be rescued at sea.

Rescue at the beach

Everyone loves playing on the beach and swimming in the sea. But swimmers and surfers can quickly be carried out to sea by strong **currents**.

Lifeguards watch out for **emergencies** on busy beaches around the world. They often watch from high up in a tower so they can see the whole beach.

What do lifeguards do?

Lifeguards keep people safe at the beach. They wear a brightly coloured **uniform** so they can be easily seen.

Lifeguards are very good swimmers. If a person is in difficulty in the water, a lifeguard can swim out to them and bring them back to shore.

What transport do lifeguards use?

Lifeguards can go out on the sea on a rescue vehicle like a jet ski. It can go very fast in **shallow** water.

Lifeguards also have vehicles with big tyres. They can drive over very soft sand, close to the sea. They can get to people who need help very quickly.

What happens when there is an emergency out at sea?

Boats may get into difficulty at sea. People on board can use a **marine** radio to call for rescue.

All boats should have **inflatable** life-rafts on board. If the boat sinks at sea, the crew can **survive** by floating on these life-rafts. They can be easily spotted by rescuers.

How are people rescued out at sea?

Lifeboats help people who are in difficulty on boats at sea. There are small, fast, **inflatable** lifeboats for rescuing people close to the shore.

There are also bigger lifeboats that can go a long way out to sea. They can go out in bad storms. They rescue people on boats that have been damaged by the wind and waves.

How do aircraft help rescue people at sea?

A helicopter can be used to search for small boats and people in the sea. It can pick up injured people and fly them quickly to a hospital.

Sea planes are sometimes used instead of helicopters to rescue people at sea. They can land on water, but cannot land if the sea is very **rough**.

What if lifeboats and planes can't get there?

Sometimes people need to be rescued from places that boats or planes can't reach. A helicopter lowers a rescuer into the water. The rescuer swims out to the person and gives them **medical** treatment.

In the Antarctic, where it is very cold, ships can become stuck in the ice. A special ice-breaking ship can go through thick ice to reach the **stranded** ship.

Making the world a safer place!

Lifeguards and lifeboat crew are very brave people. They help to make the sea safer for us.

It is important to remember the rules for staying safe at the sea:

- When you are on the beach, be aware of the tide and any warning signs.
- When you are on a boat, always wear a life jacket.
- Never try and rescue someone yourself. Always call the lifeguard or **emergency** services.

Quiz

Question 1
When is a marine radio used?
a) To call for help when a boat is in difficulty at sea
b) When someone needs help on the beach
c) On a jet ski

Question 2
Why does a lifeguard watch from a tower?
a) Because the lifeguard is shorter than other people
b) So the lifeguard can see all of the beach
c) So the lifeguard can dive into the water

Question 3
Where are ice-breaking ships used?
a) On a lifeboat
b) On the beach
c) In the Antarctic

Answers: 1a), 2b), 3c)

Glossary

current the movement of water in a river or an ocean

dangerous likely to cause harm or injury

emergency sudden and dangerous situation that must be handled quickly

inflatable can be filled with air

marine to do with the sea

medical to do with helping sick or injured people get better

rough not smooth

shallow not deep

stranded left behind

survive stay alive

uniform special clothes that members of a particular group wear

Find out more

Books

Emergency 999! Sea Rescue Services, Kathryn Walker (Wayland, 2013)

First Book of Emergency Vehicles, Isabel Thomas (A&C Black, 2014)

People who Help Us: Lifeboat Crew Member, Rebecca Hunter (Tulip Books, 2014)

Sea Rescue (Emergency Vehicles), Deborah Chancellor (Franklin Watts, 2015)

Websites

Maritime and Coastguard Agency games and information:
http://mca-kids-zone.dft.gov.uk/

Tips for keeping safe in the sea:
http://news.bbc.co.uk/cbbcnews/hi/newsid_2130000/newsid_2136800/2136861.stm

RNLI activities and information:
http://rnli.org/shorething/Pages/default.aspx

Index

Antarctic 19

beach 6, 7, 8

currents 6

helicopter 16, 18

ice breaking ship 19

jet ski 10

lifeguards 7, 8, 9, 10, 11

life raft 13

marine radio 12

safety rules 21

sea plane 17

storms 15

swimming 9, 18

tyres 11

uniform 8